MW00711306

To_____*Enjoy!*_____

From_____JIM DAVIS_____

## With lots of XOXOXOXO

# For You, With Love

Created by Jim Davis
Written by Jim Kraft and Mark Acey
Illustrated by Paws, Inc.

Andrews and McMeel
A Universal Press Syndicate Company
Kansas City

ISBN: 0-8362-0565-0

# For You,
# With Love

## Garfisms of Affection!

*L*ove is
spending
an evening
with that
special
someone.

$\mathcal{L}$ove is surviving the toughest tests ... like morning!

*L*ove is a good back scratch!

$\mathcal{L}$ove is making room under your umbrella.

*L*ove is blind ... or at least extremely near-sighted.

*L*ove is
not
always
pretty!

$\mathcal{L}$ove is having someone to teeter your totter.

Love is a little white lie ... or sometimes a big one!

$\mathcal{L}$ove is
$\mathcal{L}$one
song sung
by two.

*L*ove is sitting up with a sick friend.

ove is sharing your popcorn. True love is sharing the remote.

$\mathcal{L}$ove
is
splitting
the last
plate of
pasta.

*L*ove is the one gift you want returned.